MOVIE FAVORITES

Solos and Band Arrangements
Correlated with Essential Elements Band Method

Arranged by
MICHAEL SWEENEY

T0052813

Welcome to Essential Elements Movie Favorites! There are two versions of each selection in this versatile book. The SOLO version appears on the left-hand page of your book. The FULL BAND arrangement appears on the right-hand page. Optional accompaniment recordings are available separately in CD or cassette format. Use these recordings when playing solos for friends and family.

ISBN 978-0-7935-5959-6

HAL•LEONARD®
CORPORATION
7777 W. BLUEMOUND RD. P.O. BOX 13819 MILWAUKEE, WI 53213

00860015

From The Universal Motion Picture JURASSIC PARK

Theme From "JURASSIC PARK"

BASSOON
Solo

Composed by JOHN WILLIAMS
Arranged by MICHAEL SWEENEY

MCA music publishing

Theme From "Jurassic Park"

BASSOON
Band Arrangement

Composed by JOHN WILLIAMS
Arranged by MICHAEL SWEENEY

MCA music publishing

From CHARIOTS OF FIRE

CHARIOTS OF FIRE

BASSOON
Solo

Music by **VANGELIS**
Arranged by **MICHAEL SWEENEY**

00860015

CHARIOTS OF FIRE

BASSOON
Band Arrangement

Music by VANGELIS
Arranged by MICHAEL SWEENEY

00860015

From THE MAN FROM SNOWY RIVER

THE MAN FROM SNOWY RIVER

(Main Title Theme)

BASSOON
Solo

By BRUCE ROWLAND

Arranged by MICHAEL SWEENEY

THE MAN FROM SNOWY RIVER
(Main Title Theme)

BASSOON
Band Arrangement

By BRUCE ROWLAND
Arranged by MICHAEL SWEENEY

From The Paramount Motion Picture FORREST GUMP

FORREST GUMP - MAIN TITLE

(Feather Theme)

BASSOON
Solo

Music by ALAN SILVESTRI
Arranged by MICHAEL SWEENEY

From The Paramount Motion Picture FORREST GUMP

FORREST GUMP - MAIN TITLE
(Feather Theme)

BASSOON
Band Arrangement

Music by ALAN SILVESTRI
Arranged by MICHAEL SWEENEY

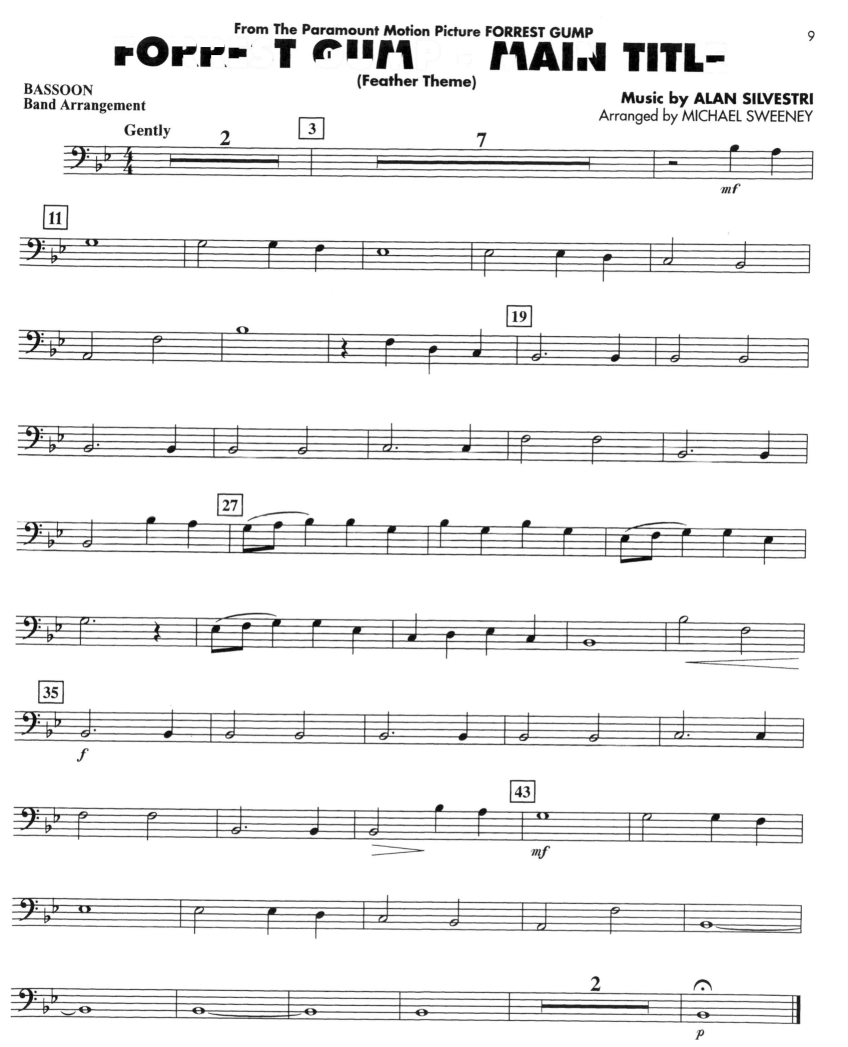

00860015

From AN AMERICAN TAIL

SOMEWHERE OUT THERE

Words and Music by JAMES HORNER,
BARRY MANN and CYNTHIA WEIL

Arranged by MICHAEL SWEENEY

BASSOON
Solo

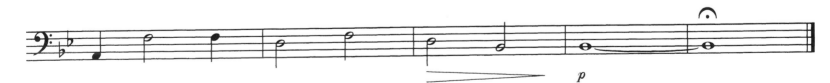

MCA music publishing

SOMEWHERE OUT THERE

BASSOON
Band Arrangement

Words and Music by JAMES HORNER,
BARRY MANN and CYNTHIA WEIL
Arranged by MICHAEL SWEENEY

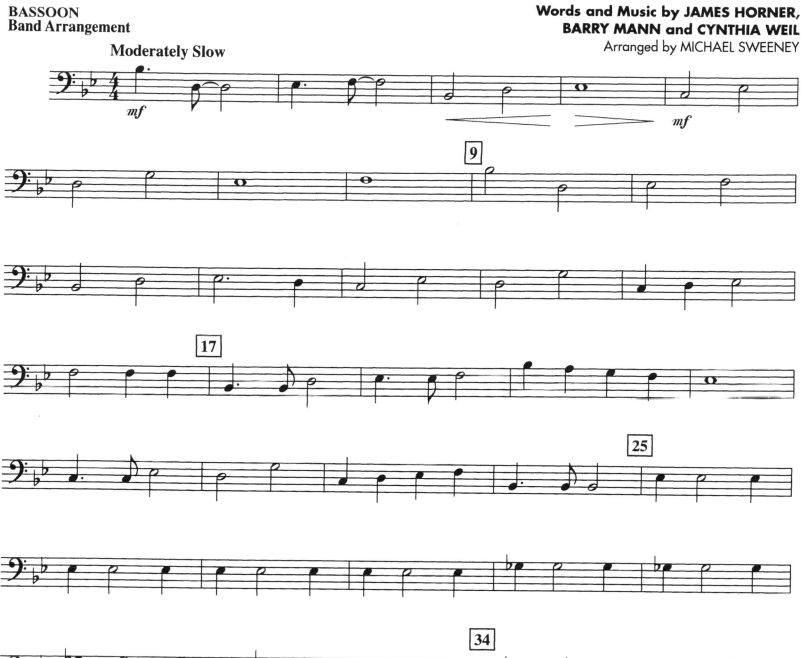

MCA music publishing

00860015

From DANCES WITH WOLVES
THE JOHN DUNBAR THEME

By JOHN BARRY
Arranged by MICHAEL SWEENEY

BASSOON
Solo

From **DANCES WITH WOLVES**

THE JOHN DUNBAR THEME

BASSOON
Band Arrangement

By JOHN BARRY
Arranged by MICHAEL SWEENEY

From The Paramount Motion Picture RAIDERS OF THE LOST ARK

RAIDERS MARCH

By JOHN WILLIAMS
Arranged by MICHAEL SWEENEY

BASSOON
Solo

RAIDERS MARCH

BASSOON
Band Arrangement

By JOHN WILLIAMS
Arranged by MICHAEL SWEENEY

From APOLLO 13
APOLLO 13
(End Credits)

By JAMES HORNER
Arranged by MICHAEL SWEENEY

BASSOON
Solo

MCA music publishing

00860015

APOLLO 13
(End Credits)

BASSOON
Band Arrangement

By JAMES HORNER
Arranged by MICHAEL SWEENEY

MCA music publishing

00860015

THEME FROM E.T. (THE EXTRA-TERRESTRIAL)

BASSOON
Solo

Music by JOHN WILLIAMS
Arranged by MICHAEL SWEENEY

MCA music publishing

THEME FROM E.T. (THE EXTRA-TERRESTRIAL)

BASSOON
Band Arrangement

Music by JOHN WILLIAMS
Arranged by MICHAEL SWEENEY

MCA music publishing

00860015

Theme From The Paramount Picture STAR TREK

STAR TREK®-THE MOTION PICTURE

BASSOON
Solo

Music by JERRY GOLDSMITH
Arranged by MICHAEL SWEENEY

STAR TREK ®-THE MOTION PICTURE

BASSOON
Band Arrangement

Music by **JERRY GOLDSMITH**
Arranged by **MICHAEL SWEENEY**

00860015

From The Universal Motion Picture BACK TO THE FUTURE

BACK TO THE FUTURE

BASSOON
Solo

By ALAN SILVESTRI
Arranged by MICHAEL SWEENEY

MCA music publishing

BACK TO THE FUTURE

BASSOON
Band Arrangement

By ALAN SILVESTRI
Arranged by MICHAEL SWEENEY

00860015

MCA music publishing